Story Writing

BY
REBECCA DYE, Ph.D.

COPYRIGHT © 2001 Mark Twain Media, Inc.

ISBN 1-58037-173-6

Printing No. CD-1394

Mark Twain Media, Inc., Publishers
Distributed by Carson-Dellosa Publishing Company, Inc.

Table of Contents

Introduction to Teachers

Including story writing in the language arts curriculum gives teachers the chance to encourage and assist students as they discover and use their imaginations. But neither competent writers nor their completed stories ever appear on demand. Taking ideas and turning them into satisfying stories with well-developed characters who, in a given setting, face and resolve some kind of conflict (move through a plot) is difficult, but rewarding work. Helping someone else try to do this is equally difficult, but rewarding work.

Teachers also have the challenge of teaching those students how to take those imaginative tales and, by applying standard English spelling and grammar rules, turn those tales into "print" ready for publishing and sharing. Research suggests that students learn best and recall longest what they want and need to know *now.* Thus, by giving enjoyable opportunities to write, we can produce students who more willingly learn and demonstrate language arts skills because the story belongs to them. They want to please their audience.

Use this text to supplement your standard language arts books. It is not meant to be used as a short-term unit in writing, but as an ongoing workshop, providing thinking/writing activities that encourage creativity. It asks students to think about stories they like to determine what typically makes a story "good." It asks student writers to consider their audience as well as their stories' purposes. It gives students sequenced activities that focus on how to create and describe interesting characters and settings. It also includes activities showing examples of how to develop satisfying story lines that include conflict and resolution. Finally, it looks at getting a story ready for in-class publishing: using editorial skills and peer review.

Introduction to Students

Humans have always had stories to tell, and we have always loved telling them and hearing them. Some of our stories are long and complicated like Thanksgiving feasts, meals that take hours to prepare, eat, and digest. Some of our stories are quick and simple, like peanut butter sandwiches made and eaten in seconds. Both are delicious in their own ways. But either way, stories meet our mind's hunger to go to new places, meet new people, and experience new challenges. Stories also let us remember and share familiar surroundings, friends, and family, and they let us relive ordinary events that left us sometimes happy, sometimes sad, and sometimes, even confused. Regardless if stories are about long ago, right now, or the future, stories are a real part of all of our lives, and good stories have some things in common.

All stories have at least one **character**: A character is a someone or a something that serves as the story's focus. Think about some of the characters in stories you have read. What is there about some characters that makes them seem so real? What kinds of things does an author do to let readers know how a character looks or thinks? What could an author do to let readers know what a character likes or doesn't like?

All stories have a **setting**, a time and place in which we find that someone or something. Think about some of your favorite stories. Where did the story happen? When did the story happen? Think about how much the story would change if it took place in a different setting (the jungle, the desert, the North Pole, or even Mars) or at a different time in history.

All stories have **conflict**, a problem the character needs to solve or resolve. And all stories have **plot**, how the character faces and goes about solving the conflict (problem). A story's conflict (problem) might appear small, but even small problems have a way of becoming huge, depending on what a character decides to do first or to never do at all.

In this book, we are going to start by doing some thinking about stories: what we know and what we expect. Then we are going to write about what we know: ourselves and our experiences. Once we feel confident with our abilities to really explain and describe the real world, we will be much more successful in creating and describing places that could be. We will also start with fairly short writing tasks, and then as we become more confident, we will tackle slightly longer ones.

We are also going to become more and more comfortable having other people read and respond to our work as we are writing, as well as when we are finished with our stories. Writers need feedback all along the story's path! Sometimes we need help generating an idea. Sometimes we need help to find a better word or a different way to say something. All writers eventually find themselves "stuck" someplace in their stories. Having a reader around can really help get your story back on track. A reader can also see things we can't see: words we've left out, mistakes in our spelling and punctuation, and words we put in that we really don't need.

Story writing requires some thinking about people, places, problems, and ways to solve those problems. You are full of stories just waiting to be created, written down, and shared. This book is to help you do just that! So roll up your sleeves, and …

Name: _____ Date: _____

Chapter One: *Don't Touch That Pencil!*

As mentioned in the Introduction to Students, a good story starts long before any words are written. A good story always starts with an idea.

Ideas come from everywhere: from what we've read, heard, or seen. Sometimes, our best ideas come from our own experiences: people we've met, places we've visited or would like to visit, and things we've done—ordinary things, as well as exciting, unusual things. After all, it is easiest to write about things that we know best.

For example, think about what you saw or experienced on your way to school today. What did you see? What did you hear? If you rode a bus, think about "bus" noises: the sound of the motor, the brakes, the door opening and closing. If you walked to school, think about neighborhood noises: voices, traffic, animals. When you walked into your school building, what did you notice first: the smell of lunch being cooked or the smell of freshly waxed floors? Chalk dust and pencil shavings, or a science experiment gone really wrong? Popcorn from last night's ballgame, or coffee from the teacher's workroom? Now jot down a few of your impressions.

On my way to school today, I …

saw _____

_____

_____

smelled _____

_____

_____

felt/touched _____

_____

_____

heard _____

_____

_____

tasted _____

_____

_____

When I walked into the building, I …

saw _____

_____

_____

Name: _____ Date: _____

Chapter One: *Don't Touch That Pencil!*

smelled _____

_____

_____

felt/touched _____

_____

_____

tasted _____

_____

_____

Sometimes story ideas are shaped by what we want our ideas (and eventually, our stories) to do. The purpose of some stories is just for fun: stories make us smile or even laugh out loud. Some make us happy by scaring us (and making us glad we are NOT part of that story) or by surprising us. Some stories teach us lessons by letting us watch characters make decisions and then face the results of those decisions. Some stories give us hope and courage.

Think about stories that you have read, heard, or seen. Jot down the names of stories you think were written to make you …

feel happy _____

_____

_____

feel scared or surprised _____

_____

_____

feel hope/courage _____

_____

_____

learn a special lesson about life. (What lesson did you learn?) _____

_____

_____

_____

Chapter One: *Don't Touch That Pencil!*

A writer has not only an idea for a story, but also thinks about what he or she wants the story to do. The writer then carefully chooses words that help tell the story just the way he or she imagines it and wants YOU (the reader) to imagine it.

Another thing a writer needs to think about is **audience**—the person or people who will be reading the story. Who might that be? Do you think that your audience will probably be preschool students or your classmates? What kinds of things interest them? What kinds of stories do they really like? Have you chosen words they will not understand? Have you chosen words they cannot pronounce? *Did you choose any words they should not pronounce?*

DANGER ... DANGER ... DANGER ... DANGER !!!!!

Because most of your written stories will be shared with your classmates and is work your teacher assigns, you need to remember and follow your class and school rules regarding language and topic. The purpose of your story **should not** be to be rude, mean, or just plain "gross" for the sake of making your audience uncomfortable. If you aren't sure about your idea, talk to your teacher before you start your story.

Writers do much thinking before they ever pick up a pencil or put even one word on the computer screen. Sometimes they draw pictures. Sometimes they jot down a few words into a notebook or "talk" their ideas onto tape. (Ideas leave as quickly as they arrive! Put it in words or pictures so you won't forget.)

I can't tell you what all writers do next, because writers do many different things once they have those ideas. Some writers like to start at the very beginning of their stories and work their way through to the last word. Some may want to write the ending first, then go back and decide how the story should start. There is simply no right or wrong way to write a story! But all writers do go back through their stories, rereading and rethinking what they said and how they said it. They add or delete words, change words, move words around, check spelling, check punctuation, ask others to read the story and make suggestions, and finally, produce a copy that makes the author happy and, hopefully, makes the audience happy, too. So at last…

Name: _____ Date: _____

Chapter One: It's Your Turn: *Writing Activity #1*

You described what you saw, smelled, felt, and tasted on your way to school, as well as what you experienced when you walked into your building. This time, try to notice details. (The floor may be brown, but is it brown like a brown paper bag or brown like chocolate cake or burned bacon? Is it made of wood, tile, or concrete? Is it rough or smooth? Cold or warm? Rectangles or squares?) Warning: Write in pencil so you can easily (and neatly) change your writing as you change your mind!

Step One: Describe …

… your desk or locker or backpack. _____

_____

_____

_____

_____

_____

… the ceiling. _____

_____

_____

_____

_____

_____

_____

_____

… the wall in the front of the room. _____

_____

_____

_____

_____

_____

Name: _____ Date: _____

Chapter One: It's Your Turn: *Writing Activity #1*

… one book on your teacher's desk. _____

_____

_____

_____

_____

_____

… your lunch. _____

_____

_____

_____

_____

… the sidewalk outside school. _____

_____

_____

_____

_____

_____

… the floor. _____

_____

_____

_____

_____

_____

_____

Name:_____ Date:_____

Chapter One: It's Your Turn: *Writing Activity #1*

… the library or media center in your school. _____

_____

_____

_____

_____

_____

… an office at your school (the principal, nurse, janitor, etc.). _____

_____

_____

_____

_____

_____

_____

Step Two:

Take a break! Close your book and DON'T even look at what you have written for AT LEAST 24 HOURS.

Step Three:

Reread your descriptions. Now make any changes you think are needed. Choose two of your descriptions to share with at least one person in your class. Have them read your work and make suggestions or comments. (Did you say too much? Too little? What was especially good?)

Step Four:

Think about the suggestions your audience made. Now is your chance to make any changes before you submit them for teacher review.

Step Five:

Your teacher will collect these descriptions or have you put them in your writing journal/folder for future use.

Name: _____ Date: _____

Chapter One: It's Your Turn: *Writing Activity #2*

This time, try to think about using a variety of words that describe …

Color   Is it … white like milk or mashed potatoes?
               Is it … red like cranberries or ketchup?

Texture   Is it … smooth like lotion or gravy?
               Is it … rough like sandpaper or stale bread?

Temperature   Is it … hot like cocoa or toast?
               Is it … cold like a popsicle or a leftover french fry?

Shape   Is it like a spoon or fork? … like spaghetti or macaroni?

Smell   Does it make you think of roses or pickle juice?

Now try describing …

… your hand. _____

_____

_____

_____

_____

_____

… your shoe. _____

_____

_____

_____

_____

_____

_____

9

Name: _____ Date: _____

Chapter One: It's Your Turn: *Writing Activity #2*

… a doughnut. _____

_____

_____

_____

_____

… a light bulb. _____

_____

_____

_____

_____

… a hammer. _____

_____

_____

_____

_____

… a pretzel. _____

_____

_____

_____

_____

_____

Name: _____   Date: _____

Chapter One: It's Your Turn: *Writing Activity #2*

… a pencil or pen. _____

_____

_____

_____

_____

… a coin or a dollar bill. _____

_____

_____

_____

_____

… a plate full of spaghetti. _____

_____

_____

_____

_____

… a banana split. _____

_____

_____

_____

_____

Reread what you have described. Which do you think is your best? Why? Go through the steps of having someone else read your work, and then have a group read and make suggestions. Save these for future use.

11

Name: _____ Date: _____

Chapter Two: *Characters*

All stories have at least one **character**. That character might be a person just like the real people we are and meet every day. In fact, it might be you! Some characters are like nobody we have ever met or want to meet. A character might be a person who lives only in our imaginations—a robot named Weasel or a tomato soup-eating monster that lives under your kitchen sink and only comes out on Tuesdays. A story character could be a pet, an animal at the zoo, a bumblebee buzzing around a petunia, a fly who was on the petunia first, or even the petunia!

Good stories have a character or characters that seem real. A writer will describe a character, but the writer will not stop there. Come to think of it, a writer will let us know a character in a story just like we come to know real people in our lives.

Think about how you would describe yourself to someone who had never seen you. If you wanted someone to recognize you in a crowd, how would you describe yourself?

_____

_____

_____

_____

_____

_____

Story characters become real when the writer lets us hear them talk, work, play, and think (out loud, letting only us hear them). Writers will even have other characters in the story discuss each other, letting us discover how other characters think and/or feel about each other as well as themselves.

Now take a look at yourself through someone else's eyes. For a few moments, trade places with someone who knows you really well. How would that person describe you?

_____

_____

_____

_____

_____

_____

Name: _____ Date: _____

Chapter Two: *Characters*

Sometimes a writer will describe a character by comparing him or her to something else.

How would you describe yourself if you were …

… a car (make, model, interior and exterior features, etc.)?

_____

_____

_____

… a kitchen appliance?

_____

_____

_____

… a musical instrument?

_____

_____

_____

… a food?

_____

_____

_____

… a sport?

_____

_____

_____

… a pet?

_____

_____

_____

Name:_____ Date:_____

Chapter Two: *Characters*

… a holiday?

_____

_____

_____

… a business?

_____

_____

_____

Maybe it is time to think about something else. Now think about someone you know very well—a friend or perhaps a family member. Briefly describe how that person looks. (Just to be on the safe side, don't use that person's *real* name. You may find it easier this way.)

_____

_____

_____

_____

_____

_____

Now, just for fun, think about that person being something other than a person. What would that person "look like" if he or she suddenly turned into …

… a vehicle (car, truck, train, etc.)?

_____

_____

_____

… a kitchen appliance?

_____

_____

_____

Name: _____ Date: _____

Chapter Two: *Characters*

… a musical instrument?

_____

_____

_____

… a food?

_____

_____

_____

… a game or sport?

_____

_____

_____

… a pet?

_____

_____

_____

… a holiday?

_____

_____

_____

… a business?

_____

_____

_____

… a plant?

_____

_____

_____

Name:_____ Date:_____

Chapter Two: *Characters*

Let's get back to the way things really are. If you were to describe how that person walks down the hall, would that person walk as if he or she were inline skating? Sneaking up to surprise someone? Dribbling a basketball? Dancing to music only he/she hears? Does this person typically have both hands jammed in his/her pockets? Does this person continually fiddle with his or her hair? Push up glasses that slide to the end of his or her nose? Describe this person simply walking down the hall at school or on a sidewalk on the way home.

_____

_____

_____

_____

_____

_____

_____

_____

Consider your friend's typical facial expression. Does your friend appear just to have woken up? Know a really funny joke? Know some strange fact? Know he/she forgot something and is desperately trying to remember it?

_____

_____

_____

_____

_____

_____

_____

_____

Name: _____ Date: _____

Chapter Two: It's Your Turn: *Writing Activity #1*

Now that you have carefully thought about how a person looks, acts, thinks, walks, and talks, put it all together. How did you originally describe yourself? Give yourself one more try. This time, using these different ways you thought about yourself (a car, a holiday, etc.), describe yourself and your personality in 30 words or less. (Choose your words carefully.) Do NOT use your real name. Call yourself either X or Y. When you are finished, your teacher will ask you to …

1) Exchange your paper with someone in your class. That person will read and suggest (in writing) how you might improve your self-description. (What could you add or remove? How else could something be said? Is there a better word? Remember, you can only use 30 words or less, and because you may want to make changes, write your description in pencil.)

OR

2) Hand in your description. The teacher will read them aloud but NOT tell who wrote them. How many in your class did you recognize from the written descriptions?

OR

3) Exchange your description (like in #1) and then, having considered and possibly having made the changes a reader suggested, hand in your description to be read aloud. (Neither the teacher nor the person who read your description will give ANY hints!!)

(Use this and the next page for your description, or if you prefer, use your own paper. Be sure you KEEP this exercise. You may need to use it later.)

_____

_____

_____

_____

_____

_____

_____

_____

_____

_____

Name:_____ Date:_____

Chapter Two: It's Your Turn: *Writing Activity #1*

_____

_____

_____

_____

_____

_____

_____

_____

_____

_____

_____

_____

_____

_____

_____

_____

_____

_____

_____

_____

_____

_____

_____

_____

_____

_____

Name: _____ Date: _____

Chapter Two: It's Your Turn: *Writing Activity #2*

Step One:

Describe someone in your family or someone who lives in your neighborhood. (You may give this person a different name if you wish.)

Let your words tell not only how this person looks, but also how this person acts, thinks, walks, and talks. Do this activity in pencil. Try to use no more than 50 words to do this, and try not to spend more than 10 to 15 minutes.

Use this space to write, or use your own paper if you prefer. (Again, be sure to keep this exercise. You might want to use it later.)

_____

_____

_____

_____

_____

_____

_____

_____

_____

_____

_____

_____

_____

_____

_____

_____

_____

_____

_____

Name:_____ Date:_____

Chapter Two: It's Your Turn: *Writing Activity #2*

Step Two:

When you find your 50 words or less, give your paper to your teacher for safekeeping until your next day of school. When you come back the next school day, your teacher will return what you wrote. You will have a chance to reread what you have written and make any changes you think are needed.

Step Three:

Now that you have NOT looked at what you have written for AT LEAST 24 HOURS, reread what you wrote and make any changes that you think are needed.

Step Four:

Have at least one person in your class read and make comments and suggestions. (Did you say too much? Too little? What was especially good?)

Step Five:

It is your last chance to make changes! Recopy your description on paper your teacher will give you.

Step Six:

Your teacher will put you into groups. Each person in the group will have a chance to read each group member's description. Discuss what parts you liked best or any suggestions that you might make to help the writer make it even better. If you agree with your reader, make those changes NOW before you forget them.

Step Seven:

Your teacher will collect these descriptions or have you put them in your writing journals/folders for future use. Whatever you do, don't just throw this away. You just might want to use it later!

Name: _____ Date: _____

Chapter Two: It's Your Turn: *Writing Activity #3*

So far, we've described people. Now try describing something that is NOT a person. You may choose a car, a place (a building, a park, etc.), a pet—something that is not a human being. Even though what you choose is not a person, it could well have a personality.

Step One:

Choose an item and describe it and its personality. (For example, if I chose to describe my toothbrush, I might begin by saying something like … My toothbrush looks like a tired old soldier in the battle against tooth decay. Its blue-striped rubber handle grips are worn thin and nearly smooth. The once bright red bristles are now nearly pink, bent and broken from marching back and forth across my molars.) Now, you give it a try. (Just don't describe your toothbrush like a tired old soldier!)

_____

_____

_____

_____

_____

_____

_____

_____

Now choose something else completely different to describe. Again, select something that is not human and attempt to describe it in ways that give it human personality.

_____

_____

_____

_____

_____

_____

_____

_____

Name: _____ Date: _____

Chapter Two: It's Your Turn: *Writing Activity #3*

Step Two:

Now that you've given two different items human personality, you must be exhausted! Give your copy of the two examples (on the page provided, or on your own paper if you prefer) to your teacher for safekeeping. When your teacher returns these on your next school day, you'll have a chance to reread what you have written and make any changes you think are needed.

Step Three:

Now that you have NOT looked at what you have written for AT LEAST 24 HOURS, reread what you wrote and make any changes you think are needed.

Step Four:

Have at least one person in your class read your two examples and make comments and suggestions. (Which do you think is better? Why? Did the author say too much? Too little? What was especially good? Did you help the author get rid of any pesky little spelling or punctuation errors?)

Step Five:

It is your turn to make changes. Decide which of your examples is your best and recopy your "fixed-up" description on paper your teacher will give you.

Step Six:

Your teacher will put you into groups. Each person in the group will have a chance to read each group member's description. Discuss what parts you liked best or any suggestions that you might make to help the writer make it even better. Take a moment to consider your audience's suggestions and, if you think your audience is right, make those changes NOW before you forget them.

Step Seven:

When you and your group feel your description is as good as it can get, give your finished copy to your teacher who will either display the work or put it in your writing journal/folder for future use.

Name: _____ Date: _____

Chapter Two: It's Your Turn: *Writing Activity #4*

If you could trade places with anyone in history, who would you like to be? What about that person interests you? Describe that person, not so much for the facts about him or her, but for the qualities you admire in that person.

_____

_____

_____

_____

_____

_____

_____

_____

_____

_____

_____

_____

_____

_____

_____

_____

_____

_____

_____

_____

_____

_____

_____

Name: _____ Date: _____

Chapter Two: It's Your Turn: *Writing Activity #4*

Step Two:

Take a break! Give your copy (on the page provided, or on your own paper if you prefer) to your teacher for safekeeping. When your teacher returns it on your next school day, you'll have a chance to reread what you have written and make any changes you think are needed.

Step Three:

Now that you have NOT looked at what you have written for AT LEAST 24 HOURS, reread what you wrote and make any changes you think are needed.

Step Four:

Have at least one person in your class read your work and make comments and suggestions. (What did you like best? Why? Did the author say too much? Too little? What was especially good? Did you help the author get rid of any pesky little spelling or punctuation errors?)

Step Five:

It is your turn to make changes. Recopy your "fixed-up" work on your own paper or paper your teacher gives you.

Step Six:

Share your work with a group of readers. Each person in the group will have a chance to read each group member's description. Discuss what parts you liked best or any suggestions that you might make to help the writer make it even better. Take a moment to consider your audience's suggestions and, if you think your audience is right, make those changes NOW (neatly) before you forget them.

Step Seven:

When you and your group feel your description is as good as it can get, give your finished copy to your teacher who will either display the work or put it in your writing journal/folder for future use.

Name: _____ Date: _____

Chapter Three: *Setting*

      All stories happen at a particular place at a particular time. This particular place and time is called the setting. The **setting** is the *where* and the *when* of a story. Setting explains what the character wears, eats, thinks, feels, and says. Setting tells the reader where the character lives, plays, and works.

      Let's begin thinking about setting by thinking about your own "space" and your own time. When it comes to space, it's all about **GEOGRAPHY**. (Remember geography—location, place, relationships within places, movement, and region?)

So, for starters, tell me where in the world you are. Describing your location involves pinpointing where you are on the surface of planet Earth—assuming that is where you are at the moment!

As precisely as you can, describe where you are sitting right now.

      I am sitting in the _____ desk in the _____

row of room #_____

(or Mr./Ms. _____'s room)

at _____ School

in/near the city of _____, which is

found at _____ degrees latitude and _____

degrees longitude.

      My city/town is located in the township/borough of _____ in the

county/parish of _____

in the state of _____

in the _____ region of the United States, which is in

the _____ Hemisphere.

Have you been there long? _____

Name: _____ Date: _____

Chapter Three: *Setting*

Now tell me about the place—the community in which your school is located. While all communities have some things in common, no two communities are exactly alike. Why do you think the town/city was started there? What are the special landmarks— buildings, parks, rivers, etc.—that distinguish it from other towns or cities in the area? How do these landmarks explain  what the community used to be like? Is now? Might be in the future? Think about the people who live in your community. What do they do for a living, find important, or generally have in common? Are there any special events or traditions in your community? Think and describe.

_____

_____

_____

_____

_____

_____

_____

_____

_____

_____

_____

_____

_____

_____

_____

_____

_____

_____

_____

_____

Name: _____ Date: _____

Chapter Three: *Setting*

From the beginning of time, people have had to learn to deal (cope) with where they were—their physical environments. For example, does climate make any difference in how or where people in your community build homes or operate businesses? Does your community have more problems dealing with tropical storms, blizzards, or earthquakes, and how does your community deal with them? Is there much new construction going on? Why are some old buildings being saved, while others are being torn down? What other changes have you noticed? New sidewalks? New highways? Fewer trees?

Briefly describe how people deal with the physical environment of your community.

_____

_____

_____

_____

_____

_____

_____

_____

_____

_____

_____

_____

_____

_____

_____

_____

_____

Name: _____ Date: _____

Chapter Three: *Setting*

Consider how people move themselves as well as their goods and services and even ideas within your community. How do you get to school, and how long does it take you? How do most people get to work, and how long does it take them? Does your community have more train tracks, airports, or parking lots? What kinds of things are made or grown in your community, and how are they transported? What kinds of things are brought into your community, and how are they transported? What (if anything) makes movement of people, goods, and/or services easy or difficult for your community?

Jot down as many ideas as you can in the space provided. Then look over your ideas and decide how you could begin to put them together in sentence form.

_____

_____

_____

_____

_____

_____

_____

_____

_____

_____

_____

_____

_____

_____

_____

_____

Name: _____ Date: _____

Chapter Three: *Setting*

Last but not least, most people would place your community in some particular region—an area having a certain characteristic or set of characteristics. Region can be simple geogra-phy: the East, West, Mid-West, North, or South. An area could be considered a region due to its climate (the tropics) or by how many people live there (urban, suburban, or rural). A region might be defined by how the majority of people make a living. Some live in the "corn belt," while others live where recreation rules. Regions in the United States have been identified by what people eat, how they tend to vote, or even the quality of air they breathe—high or low pollution.

How would you describe the region (or regions) in which you live?

_____

_____

_____

_____

_____

_____

_____

_____

_____

_____

_____

_____

_____

_____

_____

_____

_____

_____

Name: _____ Date: _____

Chapter Three: *Setting*

Where a story happens has a big impact on many of its details. Take a minute to consider how changing where the story happens would change other things in the story.

What was your favorite story when you were very young? How would the story be different if it took place in New York City, a desert, a cattle ranch, or a swamp instead of happening in the middle of a deep, dark forest? Would the main character walk to see her grandmother, or do you think she would use the subway? A surfboard? A taxi cab? A toboggan? Would she wear a red coat or a ten-gallon hat and cowboy boots?

Briefly retell a favorite story but put it in a different setting! (You may need extra paper for this one. Jot down your ideas in the space provided before you begin to write.)

_____

_____

_____

_____

_____

_____

_____

_____

_____

_____

_____

_____

_____

(Be sure to share your story with someone else. How many different places did the same story find itself? What were some of the more *interesting* changes?)

Name: _____ Date: _____

Chapter Three: *Setting*

The other part of setting is the *when* or time element. When we talk about time, we can mean

… in the middle of the night
… at the crack of dawn
… some time before lunch
… the minute school is out
… just before or after supper
… the minute you turned out the light and closed your eyes
… winter, spring, summer, or fall
… yesterday, today, or even tomorrow.

Way back in Chapter One, you wrote about what you saw and experienced on your way to school that day. (Remember, I told you that you might want to use what you wrote again!) Rewrite what you saw and experienced, but this time, pretend that you are going to school 100 years ago OR that you are going to school 100 years from now. How would things be different? (Hint: How would you be dressed? How would you travel to school? What would you eat for breakfast or lunch? What sounds might you hear?) You will need extra paper for this. Jot down your ideas in the space provided before you begin to write.

_____

_____

_____

_____

_____

_____

_____

_____

_____

_____

_____

(Be sure to share what you wrote with at least one other person in your class for comments and suggestions.)

Name: _____ Date: _____

Chapter Three: It's Your Turn: *Writing Activity #1*

Ah, yes! There is no place like home. But now think about how your house (or a particular room in your house) would be different if it were in a completely different part of the world—the middle of the desert, at the North Pole, or on an island in the South Pacific. Good luck and bon voyage! (Use the space provided to jot down as many ideas as possible. Then try a few sentences to get you started. You will probably need to do your real writing on your own paper.)

_____

_____

_____

_____

_____

_____

_____

_____

_____

_____

_____

_____

_____

_____

_____

_____

_____

_____

_____

_____

_____

_____

_____

_____

Name: _____ Date: _____

Chapter Three: It's Your Turn: *Writing Activity #1*

Step Two:

Take a break when you have completed this writing task. Give your copy to your teacher for safekeeping. When your teacher returns it on your next school day, you'll have a chance to reread what you have written and make any changes you think are needed.

Step Three:

Now that you have NOT looked at what you have written for AT LEAST 24 HOURS, reread what you wrote and make any changes you think are needed.

Step Four:

Have at least one person in your class read your work and make comments and suggestions. (Did the author say too much? Too little? What was especially good? Did you help the author get rid of any pesky little spelling or punctuation errors?)

Step Five:

It is your turn to make changes. Recopy your "fixed-up" piece on your own paper or paper your teacher gives you.

Step Six:

Your teacher will put you into groups. Each person in the group will have a chance to read each group member's description. Discuss what parts you liked best or any suggestions that you might make to help the writer make it even better. Take a moment to consider your audience's suggestions and, if you think your audience is right, make those changes NOW (neatly) before you forget them.

Step Seven:

When you and your group feel your description is as good as it can get, give your finished copy to your teacher who will either display the work or put it in your writing journal/folder for future use.

Name:_____ Date:_____

Chapter Three: It's Your Turn: *Writing Activity #2*

One of the best ways to improve our ability to describe setting (the where and when elements of a story) is to consider how things look before and after certain events.

Select and begin writing about one or two of these before/after options. (Use the space provided to jot down your ideas. You will need to provide your own paper for your "finished" piece.)

1) Describe how the doctor's or dentist's office waiting room "looks" before and after you have had your appointment. (Has the room really changed, or do you seem to look at the room in a different way?)

_____

_____

_____

_____

_____

_____

2) Describe how your kitchen looks before and after Thanksgiving dinner has been prepared.

_____

_____

_____

_____

_____

_____

3) Describe a football stadium after the championship game.

_____

_____

_____

_____

_____

_____

Name: _____ Date: _____

Chapter Three: It's Your Turn: *Writing Activity #2*

When you have completed your writing, carefully reread it to make sure it suits you. Sometimes it even helps to read it out loud. That way you can hear as well as see the words. If you tried more than one example, select the one you feel is your better piece.

Step Two:

Have at least one person in your class read and make comments. (Did you say too much? Too little? Was there really any difference in how you described the before part and the after part? What was the best part of your piece?)

Step Three:

It is your last chance to make changes. Recopy your example on paper your teacher will give you.

Step Four:

Your teacher will put you into groups. Each person in the group will have a chance to read each group member's work. Discuss what parts you liked best or any suggestions that you might make to help the writer make it even better.

Step Five:

Your teacher will collect these descriptions or have you put them in your writing journals/folders for future use.

Name: _____ Date: _____

Chapter Three: It's Your Turn: *Writing Activity #3*

Up to now, you have described real places that real people have experienced. Now try your hand at creating and describing some less (or more) than real places.

1) Describe a flower garden in which all the plants talk.

_____

_____

_____

_____

_____

_____

_____

_____

_____

_____

_____

2) Describe a zoo in which humans are on display and animals go to view them.

_____

_____

_____

_____

_____

_____

_____

_____

_____

_____

_____

Name: _____ Date: _____

Chapter Three: It's Your Turn: *Writing Activity #3*

3) Describe a school in which the students are the teachers and the teachers are the students.

_____

_____

_____

_____

_____

_____

_____

_____

_____

_____

_____

4) Describe a school in which all the students are mice.

_____

_____

_____

_____

_____

_____

_____

_____

_____

_____

Name: _____ Date: _____

Chapter Three: It's Your Turn: *Writing Activity #3*

5) Describe a cat or dog "heaven."

_____

_____

_____

_____

_____

_____

_____

_____

_____

_____

_____

_____

6) Describe your garage as your car might see it.

_____

_____

_____

_____

_____

_____

_____

_____

_____

_____

_____

_____

Name: _____ Date: _____

Chapter Three: It's Your Turn: *Writing Activity #3*

7) Describe a house made entirely of vegetables.

_____

_____

_____

_____

_____

_____

_____

_____

_____

_____

_____

_____

8) Describe a grocery store on Mars.

_____

_____

_____

_____

_____

_____

_____

_____

_____

_____

_____

_____

Name: _____ Date: _____

Chapter Three: It's Your Turn: *Writing Activity #3*

9) Describe a restaurant for chickens.

_____

_____

_____

_____

_____

_____

_____

_____

_____

_____

_____

10) Describe a library for dinosaurs.

_____

_____

_____

_____

_____

_____

 _____

_____

_____

_____

Name: _____ Date: _____

Chapter Three: It's Your Turn: *Writing Activity #3*

Step Two:

Now that you have worked your way through these tasks, take a break! Give your work to your teacher so you won't be tempted to work on it again for at least 24 hours.

Step Three:

Reread what you have written. Select two or three examples that you feel are your best work. Make any changes you think are needed.

Step Four:

Have at least one person in your class read your best work and make comments and suggestions.

Step Five:

It is your turn to make changes. Recopy your "fixed-up" work.

Step Six:

Your teacher will put you into groups. Each person in the group will have a chance to read each group member's best work. Discuss what parts you liked best or any suggestions that you might make to help the writer make it even better. Take a moment to consider your audience's suggestions and, if you think your audience is right, make those changes NOW (neatly) before you forget them.

Step Seven:

When you and your group feel your description is as good as it can get, give your finished copy to your teacher who will either display the work or put it in your writing journal/folder for future use.

Name: _____ Date: _____

Chapter Four: *Conflict and Plot*

All stories have a problem that the character (or characters) must solve or a situation the character (or characters) must face. The problem or situation is called the **conflict**. How the main character(s) go about discovering and solving the problem (or facing the situation) is called **plot**. Plot is not just the *what happened* part of a story. Plot is the *what* AND the *why* AND the *how* part of the story. No matter how simple or complicated the story's plot, no matter how funny, sad, mysterious, or surprising the plot, a good plot always seems to be reasonable when a reader gets to know the character and understands the setting and the conflict. Good plot convinces a reader that the story really could happen, and it could happen just the way the author told it.

Let's begin by thinking of the kinds of problems real people face.

Real people face problems when it comes to facing *nature or natural forces*. Sometimes weather (storms, fog, heat, and so on) is the source of the problem. Sometimes geography (mountains, rivers, deserts, and so forth) presents unexpected but interesting challenges. Sometimes, things like fire, wind, or even gravity can interfere with our plans. Plants, animals, and diseases have been known to stop us before we start.

How many stories can you recall that are based on people having to cope with nature? What kinds of human-against-nature situations have you experienced?

_____

_____

_____

_____

_____

_____

_____

_____

_____

_____

_____

_____

_____

Name: _____ Date: _____

Chapter Four: *Conflict and Plot*

Real people often have problems with other *people—groups of them.* This group could be neighbors, the opposing team, an invading army, or the people who want to build a highway through your backyard. A problem "group" could be a government as easily as it could be a gang of bullies on the playground or the jury in a courtroom.

List stories in which the character has a problem with some group. What experiences have you had involving a group of people?

_____

_____

_____

_____

_____

_____

_____

_____

_____

_____

_____

_____

_____

_____

_____

_____

_____

_____

_____

_____

_____

Name: _____ Date: _____

Chapter Four: *Conflict and Plot*

Many problems or conflicts involve just one person (perhaps you) and one other person. Two people disagree or have different ideas about what should be done or how something should happen. Conflict with just *one other person* is different than when you (or a story character) have trouble with a group.

List stories you know that are based on the problem one person has with another person. What kinds of experiences have you had?

_____

_____

_____

_____

_____

_____

_____

_____

_____

_____

_____

_____

_____

_____

_____

_____

_____

_____

_____

_____

_____

_____

Name: _____ Date: _____

Chapter Four: *Conflict and Plot*

     Sometimes a story revolves around the problem that the characters face, not with nature or natural forces, not with others, and not even one particular person. Sometimes the problem rests *inside the character himself or herself.* For example, a story character may not have any friends, but that is not the real problem. The real problem may be that the main character has a bad temper or is selfish or mean or lazy or ashamed or afraid. Perhaps the story character is too stubborn to admit that she or he is wrong. Perhaps the story character always takes the blame even when it isn't his or her fault.

List some stories that you recall having a character whose big problem is himself or herself. Have you ever experienced something like this?

_____

_____

_____

_____

_____

_____

_____

_____

_____

_____

_____

_____

_____

_____

_____

_____

_____

_____

_____

Name: _____ Date: _____

Chapter Four: *Conflict and Plot*

Now that you have identified the kinds of conflict in stories, as well as examples of the different kinds of conflict, you are ready for the next stage: plot.

Plot can be described as the process of how the conflict in a story is introduced, experienced, and if not completely solved, how it can be lived with or endured. Plot involves the steps in dealing with situations. How did you learn about the conflict? Did the author just tell you when the story began, or did you watch the character experience the problem? Did the author start the story at the very beginning and let you experience the story along with the character, or did the author start at the end of the story, then go back and explain how it all happened? Did you find yourself wanting to warn the character not to do something or to try doing something else? What kinds of things did the character try doing to solve the problem? Were the attempts successful or unsuccessful? Could you predict what was going to happen next, or were you surprised?

Think about a story you have recently read or heard or watched. What was the problem? If the character made a plan to solve the problem, did it work the first time, or did the character need to try something else? Did it ruin the story if the character didn't solve the problem with the first try, or did it make the story better?

_____

_____

_____

_____

_____

_____

_____

_____

_____

_____

_____

_____

_____

_____

_____

Name: _____ Date: _____

Chapter Four: *Conflict and Plot*

Probably the best way to write about how a character goes about solving a problem is to try to put yourself in that person's place. What would be the first thing that you would do? Hey, I said would, not should do! Since we all make mistakes, it is not unusual for us to see people in stories making all kinds of mistakes. Sometimes choices are not so much wrong turns, as twists and turns.

Here are a few "real life" situations. How might a person react? (What would you expect would happen? What would surprise you if it happened?)

1) Jill wakes up one Tuesday morning and notices that everyone in her house is still asleep. She decides to go get a drink of water and notices that the clock on the wall says it is 10:30 A.M. What does Jill do? What might she also do?

   _____

   _____

   _____

   _____

   _____

   _____

   _____

   _____

2) Al won't eat anything but peanut butter and jelly sandwiches for lunch. In his hurry to get to the bus, he happens to grab his sister's lunch bag by mistake. When lunch time comes, he opens up the bag and, instead of peanut butter and jelly, finds Janice's cheese and tuna sandwich. What does Al do? What else could he do?

   _____

   _____

   _____

   _____

   _____

   _____

   _____

   _____

Name:_____ Date:_____

Chapter Four: *Conflict and Plot*

3) Tom has $5.00 to buy a present to take to a birthday party this afternoon. He has been wanting to buy himself a video that normally sells for $10.00, but this afternoon, he notices it is on special for $4.50. What happens?

_____

_____

_____

_____

_____

_____

_____

_____

_____

_____

_____

4) John invites you to go see your favorite music group at a concert this Saturday night. When Dad comes home that evening, he says that his friend has two extra tickets for the BIG game ... this Saturday night! What happens?

_____

_____

_____

_____

_____

_____

_____

_____

_____

_____

Name: _____ Date: _____

Chapter Four: *Conflict and Plot*

5) Cameo just really hates spaghetti. She's never liked eating the stuff. It really makes her sick to her stomach. One of her classmates invites her over for supper and when she sits down, guess what they bring to the table …

_____

_____

_____

_____

_____

_____

_____

_____

_____

_____

6) Jamal wakes up one morning to discover his dog really *has* eaten his homework!

_____

_____

_____

_____

_____

_____

_____

_____

_____

_____

_____

Name: _____ Date: _____

Chapter Four: It's Your Turn: *Writing Activity #1*

Try reconstructing the steps in a real story. Tell the story of the time you were supposed to do something, but instead did something else and found yourself in a little bit of trouble. Jot down details before you begin to write the whole story.

_____

_____

_____

_____

_____

_____

_____

_____

_____

_____

_____

_____

_____

_____

_____

_____

_____

_____

_____

_____

_____

_____

_____

_____

Name: _____   Date: _____

Chapter Four: It's Your Turn: *Writing Activity #2*

Remember Jamal who woke up to find that his dog really had eaten his homework? Tell that story. (Again, jot down a few ideas you want to include before you start writing on your own paper.)

_____

_____

_____

_____

_____

_____

_____

_____

_____

_____

_____

_____

_____

_____

_____

_____

_____

_____

_____

_____

_____

_____

_____

Name:_____ Date:_____

Chapter Four: It's Your Turn: *Writing Activity #3*

One morning, you wake up to find that you have been placed in a giant, two-liter plastic bottle. Luckily for you, they (or whoever) did leave the cap off the top! Tell how you made your escape. (Jot down your ideas before you start with your full story.)

_____

_____

_____

_____

_____

_____

_____

_____

_____

_____

_____

_____

_____

_____

_____

_____

_____

_____

_____

_____

_____

(Follow the steps of having someone read your work to suggest changes. Then share your work with a small group for their reactions/responses.)

Chapter Four: *JUST A MINUTE! ...*

In many stories, characters talk to each other. Characters can either speak to each other directly (He said, "Good morning!") or indirectly (He said that he hoped I had a good day.). In the first example, I am telling you the exact words that came out of his mouth. That is called a **direct quote**. In the second example, I am telling you generally what he meant, not exactly what he said. That is an **indirect quote**, because I am just explaining or describing what he meant. When the talk is indirect, we treat it just like any other sentence.

If you tell a story in which the characters speak to each other directly, you have what is called **dialogue**, and you need to do several things a little differently.

First, you need to use quotation marks around those exact words someone says. Quotation marks are a regular part of punctuation. General punctuation rules are discussed in Chapter Six: Author Becomes Editor. But since quotation marks can be a little tricky, let's take a look at them now while we need to use them. It is much easier that way.

Use quotation marks around the exact words a character says.

I said, "You need to put quotation marks around that."

Notice that a comma is placed after *said.* Since my exact words made a complete sentence, *you* begins with a capital letter and a period follows *that.* The period in the quoted part is also the end of the whole sentence. Notice that the quotation marks go before *you* and after *that.*

Turn the same sentence around and see how things change.

"You need to put quotation marks around that," I said.

What changed? That's right. Quotation marks went around the exact words I spoke, but the word *that* was not the real end of the whole sentence. That is why the comma now goes after *that.* The whole sentence now ends with *said,* so the period goes after *said.* Always figure out where the whole sentence begins and ends, not just the exact words you are quoting.

Let's use a different quotation.

"What did you say to her?" I asked.

Because *What did you say to her?* is a question, I put a question mark inside the quotation marks. That is the only part of the sentence that is a question. The *I asked* part is not a question. It simply completes my whole sentence that contains or holds my quotation, so I put a period after *asked.* How would I treat it if I turned the sentence around? I would write it this way.

I asked, "What did you say to her?"

Chapter Four: *JUST A MINUTE! …*

I put a comma after *asked* because *I asked* introduces the exact words I used. Since *What did you say to her* is a complete sentence that ends with a question and just so happens to end my whole sentence, the question mark is all I need to use at the end of it. One punctuation mark is all I need at the end of a sentence.

We said that this is called **dialogue** because we are letting characters speak directly to each other. When we have dialogue, we need to remember to begin a new paragraph each time a different character speaks and you are telling his or her exact words. (It isn't my idea! That is just the way it works.) This is how dialogue looks in print.

Mom asked, "Do you have any homework?"

"The teacher didn't give me any," I answered.

"I can't believe that you don't have homework!" Mom laughed.

"Well, I did have some, but I finished it at school," I admitted.

So far, we have only let our speakers say one line at a time. What happens if a character has more to say than just one line? It looks like this:

"Do you have any homework?" Mom asked. "You know, we need to eat supper early tonight because we need to go to the meeting at school. You won't have much time to work when we get back."

"The teacher didn't give me any," I answered. "Well, I did have some, but I finished it at school. I didn't have any to bring home with me."

Each time the person speaking changed, I began a new paragraph. I was careful to put my quotation marks around exactly the words that *I* said and that *Mom* said. If I needed to use *Mom asked* or *I answered* at the end of a sentence, I began my new sentence with quotation marks because I was again telling the exact words coming out of a character's mouth. The speaker did not change. The speaker just started talking again.

There are more rules for using quotation marks because writers have some pretty unusual ways of letting their characters say things to each other. Still, these examples show the most common ways to use quotation marks. If you aren't sure how to use quotation marks in your work because your dialogue is different from these examples, ask your teacher OR take another look at what you wrote. How could you rewrite the dialogue to make using quotation marks a little easier?

Name: _____ Date: _____

Chapter Five: *Conclusion*

You have now begun and completed several stories. You have also had a chance to read other people's stories that were much like yours, as the stories came from the same assignments. However, did you notice that when you read your group's stories, no two stories were exactly alike?

1) How did your group members end the story in which Jamal's dog ate his homework?

A.   Your story ended when … _____

_____

_____

_____

B.   A group member's story ended when … _____

_____

_____

_____

C.   Another group member's story ended when … _____

_____

_____

_____

D.   Another group member's story ended when … _____

_____

_____

_____

In your groups, discuss (and be ready to discuss with the whole class):

2) Which group member had the story with the most unusual ending? Why?

_____

_____

_____

_____

_____

_____

Name: _____ Date: _____

Chapter Five: *Conclusion*

3) Which group member wrote a story with the most interesting details? Why?

_____

_____

_____

4) Which story was the most complicated? Explain.

_____

_____

_____

5) Think about how each story had a *purpose:* a reason why the story happened as it did. Was there a story that had Jamal learning some kind of lesson? (Don't leave homework on the floor! Don't forget to feed the pets!) Was there a story that was simply funny? Was there a sad story? Did *you* have a purpose behind *your* story? What was that purpose, and how difficult was it to achieve that purpose?

_____

_____

_____

_____

6) If you could rewrite your story, what changes would you make?

_____

_____

_____

_____

_____

_____

_____

_____

_____

Name: _____ Date: _____

Chapter Five: *Conclusion*

Consider the story in which you all found yourselves in two-liter plastic bottles.

7) How did the people in your group explain their getting into the bottles?

_____

_____

_____

_____

_____

8) How did the people in your group explain their getting out of the bottles?

_____

_____

_____

_____

_____

9) If you could change your story in any way, how would you change it?

_____

_____

_____

_____

_____

_____

_____

10) What would you say is the purpose behind your story? (Teaching a lesson? Just for fun?)

_____

_____

_____

_____

Chapter Five: *Conclusion*

However you choose to end your story, it needs to make sense with everything else that happens in the story. For example, it wouldn't be such a good idea to suddenly have an alien spaceship land in your main character's backyard and kidnap him or her to end the story if the story was about how your main character finally learned to swim. *What does the spaceship have to do with learning how to swim?* Also, it would not make sense to have a story ending with your best friend moving 2,000 miles away and then saying something like "… and they lived happily ever after." Yes, you might eventually live happily ever after, but I bet it would take a while for you to feel very happy about it.

Must every story have a happy ending?

Must every story have an ending?

It is important to remember that in real life, real people like you and me don't always solve every problem or solve every problem completely. Sometimes we only figure out a way to postpone solving it or realize that perhaps the problem wasn't so big after all. Sometimes, however, the problem is just as big and bad as we thought!

Since we can't solve every problem we face, we don't have to make our characters solve every problem they face. But we do need to end the story in a way that your reader will think, "Well, it probably could have happened that way," or "If I had been in that situation, at that time, and in that place, I might have done the same thing," or even "I know just how that person feels."

Chapter Six: *Author Becomes Editor*

An author has one basic job: to create and tell (out loud or in print) a story. An editor has two jobs to do.

The editor's first job is to make sure that when a story is written down, that story really is a story. A story must tell how characters discover and work through situations. A story must have a beginning that gives the readers some idea about where the story happens, when the story happens, and who is involved in making the story happen. The story will need to have a "middle" part in which people or characters in the story identify the conflict and choose ways to solve or work through the conflict. That is the part that can be complicated, because not everything happens the way we expect. The story must also have some kind of ending: the problem may be solved completely, not at all, or just enough to get by for a little while. The editor reads the story and tries to give the writer the suggestions about changes that a group of readers might feel are needed.

Sometimes editors suggest that the writer take out parts that are confusing or do not really add to the story. Sometimes editors suggest that the writer add details because as it is, the story just seems a little empty in spots, or it doesn't make sense. Sometimes editors suggest that the writer has included too many ideas or made the story so complicated that the reader will be too tired to want to finish the story. The editor is NOT there to rewrite a story, but he or she is there to help the author figure out the best way to tell the story.

The editor must also be sure that once the story is published (is ready for an audience), the story measures up to many different rules: spelling rules, grammar rules, and punctuation rules.

Spelling Rules

The rule is that each word is important. Let one little letter get out of place and you could say something completely different from what you had intended to say. For example, there is a big difference between a person wearing a *fur* coat (one made of animal skin) and a coat made from the branches of a tree—a *fir* coat. A story that happens in a *desert* is very different from a story that takes place in a *dessert*. The dictionary is an important friend to authors and editors!

Grammar and Punctuation Rules

Generally speaking, grammar is how we put words together to form sentences—complete thoughts—to share ideas. When you study English or any language, you learn that there are certain patterns that people follow to make sure that the writer and the reader understand each other. Punctuation is not just using little marks to fill in spaces around words. Each little punctuation mark has meaning, and using the wrong punctuation mark can change the meaning of your entire sentence.

Following these rules is as important as following any rules. Just imagine how impossible baseball or soccer or basketball would be if there were no rules. Think how upset people would become if, for some reason, someone decided to change the rules in the middle of playing the game!

59

Chapter Six: *Author Becomes Editor*

Rules for writing are just as necessary as rules for any game. For example, we begin our sentences with capital letters and end them with one of three kinds of punctuation marks: a period, a question mark, or an exclamation point. We tend to group related sentences together into paragraphs, and whenever we begin a new paragraph, we indent it: begin it on a new line and place the first word slightly to the right of the left margin. (You will indent, unless your teacher lets you use block form.) Remember, the rules are written to describe how most readers expect us to write so we can be best understood. If we confuse or lose our readers in a jungle of words, we've cheated ourselves as well as the readers.

What are the rules your teacher expects you to know and understand? Some teachers have these written on posters hung on the walls for easy reference. Some teachers have these on a sheet of paper to remind students as they write or for students to use when they act as their own editors.

If your teacher does not have a set of rules for you to use, I would suggest that you try these. Ask yourself …

1. Have I written everything in complete sentences?

2. Does each sentence begin with a capital letter and end with a period, a question mark, or an exclamation point?

3. Have I used commas where they need to be?

    *   … after a group of words introducing the rest of my sentence.
        When we finally arrived at the party, I was too tired to eat.
        Because I didn't go to the party, I didn't win a prize.
        After the concert, we went out for pizza.

    *   … between sentences joined by *and, or, nor, but, for,* or *yet.*
        I told her not to try it, but she decided to do it anyway.
        Amos was shocked by the news, and Tracy was amazed.
        You can choose to go to the mall, or you might just stay at home.

    *   … between words describing the same word.
        It was a cold, dark, miserable night.
        The cookies were crisp, sweet, and delicious.
        The book was interesting, challenging, and short.

    *   … between items in a series.
        I was supposed to buy soap, paper plates, milk, bread, and salt.
        Renate had lived in Rome, London, Madrid, Seattle, and Rolla.
        John ate a hot dog, an ice cream cone, popcorn, and a brownie.

60

Chapter Six: *Author Becomes Editor*

- … between the city and state, in addresses, with certain names, between the day and date, etc.

  Los Angeles, California
  Pittsburgh, Pennsylvania

  I live at 1234 Anystreet, Owensville, Missouri.
  The President lives at 1600 Pennsylvania Ave., Washington, D.C.

  His uncle is Jason Oreo, Jr.
  Allen had an appointment with John Keller, M.D.

  Monday, January 15, 2001
  Friday, April 1, 1983

There are more rules for using commas. These are the ones that people use most often; however, if you have studied more rules, you will be expected to use them and use them properly. Check your language arts book! Ask your teacher!

4. If I used dialogue, did I use quotation marks correctly?

5. Are there any words that I am NOT sure I have spelled correctly?

6. Have I read my work out loud to make sure I have not left out any words?

7. Have I had several others read my story to make sure it does what I planned for it to do? Do they think everything in my story makes sense?

8. Is my story neatly written or word-processed? (If you wrote in pencil, are your erasures clean or smeared? Were you supposed to skip lines? If you wrote in ink, were you supposed to use blue or black ink and NOT red or green ink? Did you dot each *i* and cross each *t,* or did you cross each *i* and dot each *t* ?)

9. Were there any other instructions I was to follow? (Did my teacher say I was to have this in a folder? Was I supposed to include artwork?)

10. Will I be proud to put my name on my story?

Story Writing

Chapter Seven: *It's Your Turn! Ideas for Future Use*

Chapter Seven: *It's Your Turn! Ideas for Future Use*

Here are some more ideas for stories you might like to try.

1. Imagine what would happen if, suddenly, your dog (or cat) began to talk. Your pet will talk only to you—no one else.

2. You sit down and begin to read a book you just checked out from your local library. When you turn the page to start the second chapter, you find two $50 bills and a note telling where someone hid the rest of the money.

3. Instead of buying a cake for Mom's birthday, you and your younger brother or sister decide to make one using a recipe in one of her cookbooks. The only other cooking you have ever done is making a peanut butter and jelly sandwich, and that didn't turn out well.

4. It is a beautiful day, and you decide to ride your bike over to a friend's house. As you near the last turn, you notice that they are repaving the street. You must make a detour.

5. One day while cleaning up your closet, you find a tiny door. When you turn the door-knob, …

6. You are cleaning away leaves from your yard. Suddenly, you hear your rake striking something that sounds like metal. When you lean down and take a close look, you discover …

7. It is your first trip to the zoo.

8. Your cousins are coming for their first visit. They plan to stay a week.